Thirty Days of Thoughts About the Holidays

Rev. Dr. Kevin T. Coughlin Ph.D.

KTC Publishing Phase IIC Coaching, LLC

This book is a work of nonfiction.

Except where noted; names, characters, places, and incidents are the product of the author's imagination or are used fictitiously. Any resemblance to actual events, locales, or persons, living or dead is coincidental.

First Printing

Printed in the United States of America

ISBN 978-0-9977006-0-2 (paperback)

Introduction

Thirty Days of Thoughts for the Holidays is a collection of thoughts, memories, and lessons learned over a lifetime of Holidays with and without family and friends. Best-selling author Rev. Dr. Kevin T. Coughlin Ph.D. shares his thoughts, heart, and soul as you travel a journey of thirty days of his thoughts, memories, and lessons learned over his lifetime with him.

You can expect this thoughtful little book to bring up some feelings and memories from the Holidays during your lifetime. This honest, heartfelt look at life and some of the truths learned by the author are priceless.

The Holidays can be a tough time of year for some people, depending on their life situations. If nothing else, perhaps this literary pearl will make us all more aware of the human condition that impacts us all at certain times of our lives.

There's nothing like a good book, a warm drink, a comfortable chair in front of a glowing fireplace on a cold winter's night, where that book makes us think, feel, and want to be a better human being.
Thirty Days of Thoughts for the Holidays is the author's ninth book.

PLEASE VISIT www.theaddiction.expert for other books written and published by Rev. Dr. Kevin T. Coughlin Ph.D., there you can join his mailing lists for advanced notice on his next books, trainings, and live events.

Day One

"I remember all of the colorful blinking lights, the crisp winter air, and the hustle and bustle of people everywhere. People always seemed so much nicer around the Holidays. Growing up in New England, I saw more than my fair share of snow as a boy. I remember snowball fights, snow forts, snowsuits and gigantic rubber boots, mittens, and those winter hats that looked like bank robber masks. My older brother and I would return home soaked to the skin after an afternoon of play in our own snow fantasy land."

Day Two

"Hearing the Holiday music being played on the radio, in stores, and in the streets of small towns always seemed to cheer me up as a child. My mother was studying to sing opera. When I was very young she would sing to me; she had the voice of an angel. My mother always tried to make the Holidays so nice for the family."

Day Three

"Secret Santa in school could be fun; however, awkward; depending on who the other person was that was picked out of the hat. The presents were usually not very good ones. I never let most people in school get close to me. When I look back now, I realize that I wasted so many years trying to be a tough guy and protect my ego. The truth is, I was scared to death of other people. I was scared that people wouldn't like me, scared of rejection."

Day Four

"People were always extra generous around the Holidays; I always made bigger tips, got better bonuses, it was a great time of year for younger people who need money. When I was a senior in high school, I was bartending at night to make extra money, my family lived in a very wealthy town; however, we were not wealthy. Both my parents worked most of their lives to support our family. I was very blessed to have such loving, caring, hardworking parents."

Day Five

"I think my pets growing up always enjoyed the Holidays; they got lots of treats to eat, funny costumes, and lots of love and attention. I loved watching them play in the snow. I love dogs, there is something about them. My dogs have made a wonderful difference in my life."

Day Six

"My favorite homes were the ones with fireplaces, where we could have glowing fires when the relatives came over to celebrate at the Holidays. I've always loved indirect lighting since childhood. I don't care for bright lighting, even when I managed restaurants, I always utilized indirect lighting and candles."

Day Seven

"My dad always used to insist on a real tree in the living room for the Holidays; the whole family would decorate the tree and dad would put the star or angel on the top. Dad would have to wire the tree to the wall because we usually had at least one cat in the house over the years, and more than one tree had been climbed by our furry friends. We all loved the way that the house smelled with a real tree inside; however, we had to be careful that it had lots of water so that it wouldn't become a fire hazard."

Day Eight

"Christmas Eve always seemed magical to me as a child, the indirect lighting, the fireplace, the wonderful foods and treats, the presents, having relatives over, and waiting for Santa to arrive. The stories the relatives would tell always made the family laugh; they had some really funny stories from the past."

Day Nine

"Thanksgiving always seemed like a ton of work for a few minutes of feasting. I remember my dear mother waking up at 4AM to start the turkey and the other cooking, and then later in the morning trying to get the family ready for church. We'd watch football or a good movie after the feast and then the best part of all, the turkey sandwiches at dinnertime! I don't know what it is about those turkey sandwiches with mayo, cranberry sauce, stuffing, and turkey on a roll!"

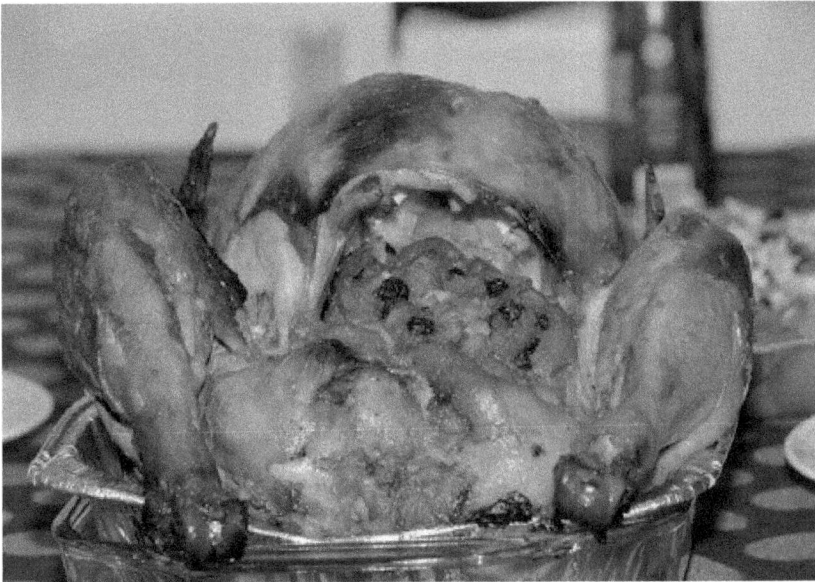

Day Ten

"It always seemed like the whole family would fall asleep after the Thanksgiving feast; it must have been the turkey! I suppose it could have been consuming all those calories in such a short period of time, and the amount of sugar in the desserts, it's no wonder that everyone crashed out for a while."

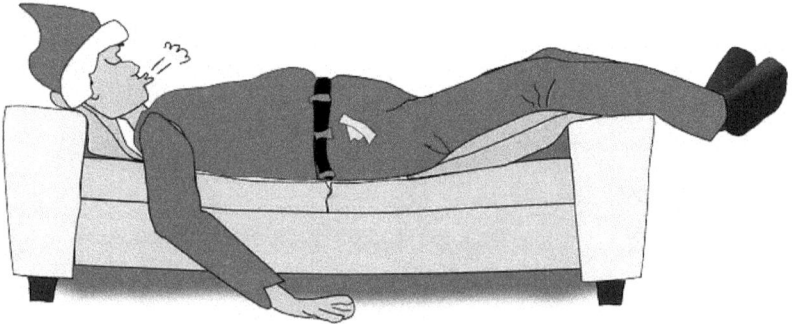

Day Eleven

"Thanksgiving could be a tough Holiday to get through; when all the family got together, at times the feathers would fly! It would have helped at all Holidays if we all remembered what we were gathering to celebrate. I really don't care for all of the commercialization of the Holidays; I like to keep it simple and the real meaning of each Holiday."

Day Twelve

"I always thought that the best presents were ones that took great thought and were made by the person giving the gift. To me the worst thing a person can do is hand someone cash without any thought; it's like saying, I didn't put any thought into you at all, or you're not important!"

Day Thirteen

"I learned one Thanksgiving that grandmothers should not consume alcohol in large amounts at the feast or the feathers will fly and the family will cry! Granny got so drunk that she threw the turkey across the room! I can't remember what we had for dinner, but it wasn't turkey."

Day Fourteen

"I used to love listening to my uncles, grandparents, and parents tell stories at Holiday get-togethers. Everyone would tell stories and laugh and laugh, good times! I really learned to listen to and respect my elders, they have so much wisdom and know how."

Day Fifteen

"When you're young, you don't realize how selfish and self-serving you are at the Holidays. At least, I didn't! I had a great deal to learn as a young man."

Day Sixteen

"Some years my parents had more money than other years. I remember as a small child the mountain of gifts that were waiting under the tree for the kids on Christmas morning some years, and other years we struggled."

Day Seventeen

"In later years, my parents didn't have much money one year; I had saved up to send them on a round trip to Aruba. I left an envelope on the mantle of their fireplace Christmas Eve. They were so surprised! A great memory."

Day Eighteen

"We had neighbors when we were growing up that loved to decorate their houses for the Holidays; God only knows what their electric bills were! They reminded me of the movie National Lampoon Christmas."

Day Nineteen

"One year my grandmother's sister came to visit from Scotland for Christmas. Her name was Ida; she was in her late seventies. I had the pleasure of being her personal bartender at the bold age of thirteen. The poor thing didn't know what hit her! She was bombed for her entire visit! I don't know if she even remembered her visit to the states."

Day Twenty

"As I started to get older, I started to get bored hanging around the Holiday gatherings with family." Now I realize that it was my attitude and that I should have cherished every minute; however, I was selfish back then! Today I would give anything to have that time back to spend with my family and friends."

Day Twenty-One

"I realized when I added alcohol to my Holiday it became very different, very different! At first, I got a warm fuzzy feeling and everything felt like it fit just right, it was all downhill from there."

Day Twenty-Two

"I always liked shopping a few days before the Holiday; I could take advantage of the sales and get everything done at once. The truth is, I hate to shop in stores! I love Amazon.com now because I can do all my shopping online!"

Day Twenty-Three

"I realized that you don't realize what you have until it's gone! Holidays with family as a child were wonderful, magical, and so very special. When we lost mom unexpectedly five years ago, it shocked me in such a powerful way that I don't know if I will ever totally be all right! I know that Holidays will never be the same without her. Dad is eighty-six now so, for the most part, it's him and I. It's very important to spend the time we have together."

Day Twenty-Four

"I realized that Holidays aren't about food, presents, and decorations; Holidays are about family, friends, and love. Holidays are about sharing time together, experience, and life! Holidays are a spiritual time."

Day Twenty-Five

"I realized that there is no room for drugs or alcohol at Holiday celebrations and certainly no need for them. When you have family and friends with you at the Holidays, you have everything that you need! We say high on life!"

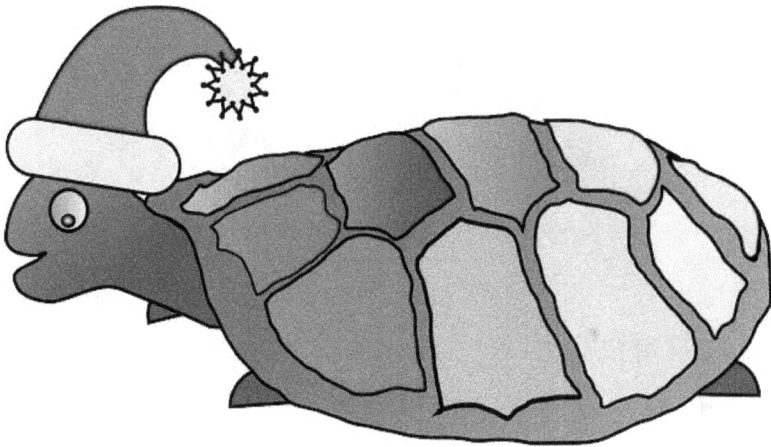

Day Twenty-Six

"I learned with age that the greatest gift is giving to others and being of service to others! When we do these things we give unconditional love the best we can. I believe that love is the power that heals us."

Helping Others is not a Choice It is a Purpose.

Day Twenty-Seven

"I found out that life and the Holidays are not about me being entertained; it's about me being grateful for all that I already have, all that I've been freely given by others over my lifetime. An attitude of gratitude goes a long, long way in life."

Day Twenty-Eight

"I learned that I can't take things and people for granted, nothing lasts forever. That we all need to enjoy the moment. The only constant in this world is change!"

Day Twenty-Nine

"I found out that the older you get, the quicker the Holidays come and many of those loved ones are now memories, precious memories! I learned to find joy in the simple things and to take faith. Time doesn't wait for any of us and it plays funny little tricks on us. You older folks know what I mean, let's let the younger ones find out on their own!"

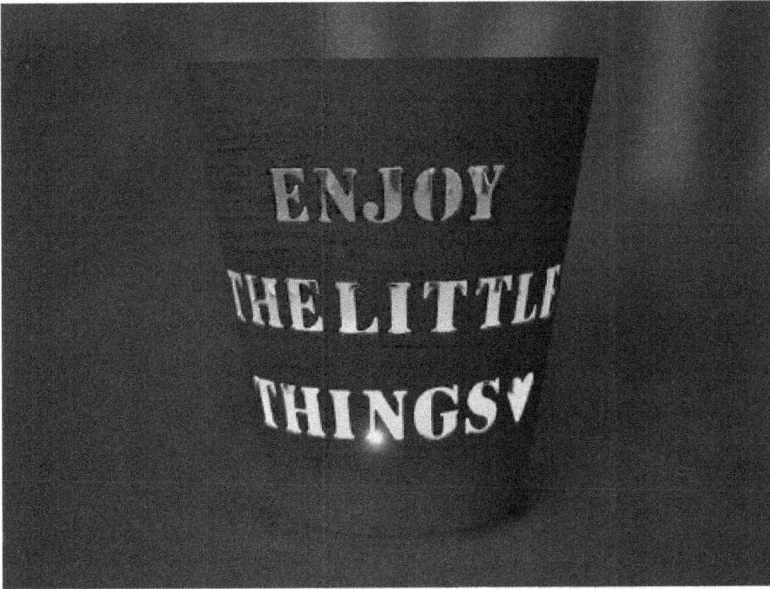

Day Thirty

"I learned that every day is a Holiday and should be treated that way. We should treat friends, family, and people in general with the same love and understanding every day that we would on a Holiday! All that really, matters in the end, is family and friends, and real love. Happy Holidays Friends, if no one else told you that they love you today, please let me be the first, I love you today!"

Rev. Dr. Kev's Publication Credits

KTC Publishing Phase IIC Coaching, LLC Amazon.com
Recovery & Life Coaching; The Official Workbook for Coaches
and Their Clients. Co-Author Dr. Cali Estes 2016 #1 Best-Seller
Amazon.com Top 100 Best-Seller List
KTC Publishing Phase IIC Coaching, LLC Amazon.com
*Addictions: What All Parents Need to Know to Survive the Drug
Epidemic.* 2016 Made the Amazon.com Top 100 Best Seller list.
KTC Publishing Phase IIC Coaching, LLC Amazon.com *If You
Want What We Have; A Journey Through the Twelve Steps of
Recovery Workbook and Manual* 2015 Made the Amazon.com
Top 100 Best Seller list.
KTC Publishing Phase IIC Coaching, LLC Amazon.com *In The
Sunlight of the Spirit* Workbook and Manual 2015
KTC Publishing Phase IIC Coaching, LLC Amazon.com *We
Can; A Collection of Poetry, A Journey Through Addiction and
Recovery 2016*
KTC Publishing Phase IIC Coaching, LLC Amazon.com *We
Can 2; A Collection of Poetry, A Journey Through Addiction and
Recovery 2016*
KTC Publishing Phase IIC Coaching, LLC Amazon.com *We
Can 3; A Collection of Poetry, A Journey Through Addiction and
Recovery 2016*
Tumbleweeds; Feather Books Poetry Series a Book of Poetry
Written by Rev. Kevin T. Coughlin Feather Books England May
2002 (In Memory of DeWitt)
Wayne Independent Newspaper Honesdale, PA
News Eagle, Hawley, PA
Reading Eagle, Reading, PA Berks & Beyond
www.addictsrehab.com
My RecoveryRadio.com Host Kent Paul Sept. 11[Th], 2016
Interview
BBS Radio Poetry reading
Blog Talk Radio - Interviews
The Serenity Show - Interview
Passion Diva Radio- Interview
www.sacredearthpartners.com - Interview
The Broken Brain (Blog Talk Radio) - Interview

www.eatingdisorderhope.com
Keys to Recovery Newspaper Beth Dewey CEO
www.keystorecovery.com
All 4 Ur Addiction Recovery Referral Resource Guide Jenny
Clark Owner
Tripadvisor.com
MindBodyNetwork
Grieving Behind the Badge Peggy Sweeny Founder
www.theaddictsmom.com
In Recovery Magazine
The Sober World Magazine
The Soberworld.com
Shout My Book
Bookgoodies.com
Goodreads
Book Reader Magazine
Awesomegang.com
www.christiancoaches.com
NEWS CHANNEL 10 EYEWITNESS NEWS
CHANNEL.COM
KHQQ6 ABC NEWS
ABC EYEWITNESS NEWS 8 KLKN-TV
FOX14 NEWS AT 9
Erie News Now
NTV Nebraska.TV ABC
Western Mass News Channels 3 ABC 40 Fox 6
ABC9 KTRE
7 KLTV ABC
Fox 19 Now
KXNEWC Eyewitness News
12 WSFA ABC
ABC 6 News WLNE TV
100.7 KFM BFM
Fox 5 KVVU-TV Local Las Vegas
13 WTHR COM Indians News ABC
Eyewitness News 3 WFSB.COM
Fox 12 Oregon
WDRB.COM
Fox29 WFFX.COM

WETV San Diego
HAWAII News Now
Marketers Media
WALB News 10 ABC
Tristate Update.com 13 News WOWK
AM760
WMBF ABC News
KCEN HD ABC KCENTV.COM
WECT6 ABC News
Eyewitness News3 WFSB.COM
WLOX ABC BOUNCE Eyewitness News
Eyewitness News 8
CBS8.COM
News channel 6 KAUZ
SPROUT News
12 Eyewitness News KFVS
KEYC MANKATO News 12 CBS & FOX LOCAL NEWS
3 WRCB TV ABC COM
KNDO 23 NBC
KNDU 25 NBC
The Aurorean, Encircle Publications 1998 Poetry and Essays
Joel's House Publications 1998-2005 Poetry and Essays
Our Journey 1998-2005 Poetry
The Poetry Explosion, The Pen 1999-2003 Poetry
Apostrophe 1998 Poetry
Nuthouse Twin Rivers Press 1998 Poetry
The National Library of Poetry 1998
Lines N' Rhymes 1998 Poetry
The Poetry Church Feather Books
England. Anthology John Hunt Publications 1999 Poetry
A Tapestry in Time. 1999 Poetry Book 18 Poems
Connecticut Department of Mental Health and Addiction Services
The Webster Times 1999 Poetry
The Angel News 1999 Poetry
The Skater won The Editor's Choice Award September 1999 (Our Journey)
The Blind Man's Rainbow 1999 Poetry
Arnazella 2001 Poetry

Feather Books, The Poetry Church 1998-2002
The American Dissident 2002 Poetry
The Good Shepherd Poetry 2002
Ya ' Sou Magazine Essays and Poetry
Colt. Winner Editor's Choice Award Contest Literally Horses 2002
Goodbye My Friend Read on the Radio Rhyme and Reason UBC Europe & the UK September 2001 Read on the Radio in Europe and the UK as a Tribute to those lost on September 11th bombings. My poem was read over the radio for many days.
Tumbleweed Read on BBC Radio in England 2001
Published by Feather Books
Notified by John Waddington Feather that Tumbleweed had been read on BBC Radio in England on Several Occasions.
Stanwich Congregational Flyer Poetry
University of Scranton Panuska College of Professionals Essay 2002
Scranton University 2002 Poetry
The River Reporter Newspaper 2002 Poetry
Unity Community News 2002 Poetry
The Poetry Corner Angelfire.com Poetry
The Poet's Market 2002 Poetry
The Poetry Church England 2003 Poetry
Cover of Wayne Independent News 2003 Poetry
Nomad's Choir 2003 Poetry
Written a series of 9 course manuals for a coaching recovery curriculum. 2014-2015
www.addictedminds.org 2015-2016 Articles Matthew Steiner
www.soberservices.com 2015 Articles
http://fromaddict2advocate.blogspot 2016 Articles Marilyn Davis
LinkedIn 2014-2016 Articles
Two Drops of Ink S.W. Biddulph 2015- 2016 Poetry/ Articles
The Addict's Mom 2016 Articles Blog
Ghostwriter Articles/ Content2014-2016
KEITV12 : The Kingdom Hour- InterviewBlogTalkRadio The Kingdom Hour- Interview

About The Author

Rev. Dr., Kevin T. Coughlin Ph.D., DCC, DDV, DD, IMAC, NCIP is an International Master Coach, trainer, #1 best-selling author, writer, poet, speaker, a Diplomate Christian counselor, and therapist, he is Board Certified in Family, DevelopRemental, Alcoholism, Substance Abuse, and Grief Counseling, the Reverend is a NCIP interventionist, a Domestic Violence Advocate, Associate Professor for DCU, a Provincial Superintendent (to be consecrated a Bishop in 2016) and so much more; he is an expert in the field of Addiction and Recovery.

He was a Founder and Board Member of a Residential Recovery Facility New Beginning Ministry, Inc. and is President and CEO of Phase IIC Coaching, LLC., The Program Director for The Addictions Academy, and the former Editor in Chief for Addicted Minds & Associates. The Reverend has over forty-seven years of experience with the AA program.

He has been working in the addiction recovery field for almost two decades, has helped thousands of individuals and their families overcome all types of addictions, substance abuse, alcoholism, process addiction, shame and guilt, relationship and communication problems, anger management, inner healing, self-image, interventions and much more. He is a published author and has published thousands of poems and articles published throughout the United States and other Nations, he has been interviewed on numerous radio talk shows, television, published in magazines, newspapers, books, and online publications; he has been featured on ABC, CBS, FOX, NBC, and the BBC in the UK. Rev. Kev is a former State, National & World-Champion Powerlifter, and still, holds several records. He loves to write, read, teach, listen to music, and spend time with people and dogs. His parents are his heroes.

Rev. Dr. Kev's Social Media Accounts

https://www.goodreads.com/author/show/14874631.Kevin_Coug
hln

About Me Links:

https://about.me/ktc1961/

http://ilikeebooks.com/if-you-want-what-we-have/

http://awesomegang.com

www.amazon.com/Rev.-Kevin-
TCoughlin/e/B01AF6AAAI/ref=ntt_dp_epwbk_0

http://www.barnesandnoble.com/w/addictions-what-all-
parents-need-to-know-to-survive-the-drug-epidemic-rev-dr-
kevin-t-coughlin-phd/1124049106?ean=9780997700695

http://www.barnesandnoble.com/w/in-the-sunlight-of-the-
spirit-rev-dr-kevin-t-
coughlin/1124049139?ean=9780997700671

http://www.barnesandnoble.com/w/if-you-want-what-we-
have-rev-dr-kevin-t-
coughlin/1124049130?ean=9780997700688

http://mybookplace.net/in-the-sunlight-of-the-spirit-a

Facebook
1. Kevin Coughlin:
   https://www.facebook.com/profile.php?id=100008449955607
2. My Group, Resources for those suffering from addiction and their families:
   https://www.facebook.com/groups/resourcesforthosesufferingfromaddiction/
3. RevKev The Addiction Expert:
   https://www.facebook.com/RevKev/?fref=ts

LinkedIn
1. Rev. Dr. Kevin T. Coughlin PhD
   https://www.linkedin.com/in/revkevnetwork

Google+
1. Kevin Coughlin
   https://plus.google.com/112400908736308001821/posts
   My Group: The Recovery Community Family and Friends:
   https://plus.google.com/communities/113521225141112811207

Pinterest
1. Kevin Coughlin: https://www.pinterest.com/ktc1961/
2. My Group Board: Recovery We Can
   https://www.pinterest.com/ktc1961/recovery-we-can/

Tumblr
1. https://www.tumblr.com/blog/revkevsrecoveryworld

Instagram
theaddiction.expert

My Websites:
1. www.revkevsrecoveryworld.com
2. theaddiction.expert

3. theaddiction.guru

Rev. Kev's Goodreads Link:
-spirituality-training-manual-and-workbook-by-kevin-
coughlin
**Thank you for reading my work! If you enjoyed my
book, would you consider reviewing it on Amazon.com?
We would appreciate your help in getting the word out
on how helpful this book. Thank you so much!**